First World War
and Army of Occupation
War Diary
France, Belgium and Germany

4 CAVALRY DIVISION
Divisional Troops
Royal Army Service Corps
Divisional Supply Column (89 Company A.S.C.)
1 January 1917 - 31 March 1918

WO95/1158/11

The Naval & Military Press Ltd
www.nmarchive.com
Published in association with The National Archives

Published by

The Naval & Military Press Ltd

Unit 10 Ridgewood Industrial Park,

Uckfield, East Sussex,

TN22 5QE England

Tel: +44 (0) 1825 749494

www.naval-military-press.com

www.nmarchive.com

This diary has been reprinted in facsimile from the original. Any imperfections are inevitably reproduced and the quality may fall short of modern type and cartographic standards.

© **Crown Copyright**
Images reproduced by permission of The National Archives, London, England, 2015.

Contents

Document type	Place/Title	Date From	Date To
Heading	WO95/1158/11		
Heading	1917-18 4th Cavalry Division Divl Supply Column Jan 1917-Mar 1918 89 Coy ASC From IInd Cav Div Box 1173 To 17 Corps Box 949		
Heading	War Diary of 4th Cavalry Divisional Supply Column. From 1st January 1917 To 31st January 1917		
War Diary	Fressenneville	01/01/1917	31/01/1917
Heading	War Diary of 4th Cavalry Supply Column From 1.2.17 To 28.2.17 Volume 7		
War Diary	Fressenneville	01/02/1917	28/02/1917
Heading	War Diary of 4th Cavalry Supply Column From 1.3.17 To 31.3.17 Volume 8		
War Diary	Fressenneville	01/03/1917	31/03/1917
Heading	War Diary of 4th Cavalry Supply Column From 1st April 1917 To 30th April 1917 Volume 9		
War Diary		01/04/1917	30/04/1917
Heading	War Diary of 4th Cavalry Supply Column From May 1st 1917 To June 30th 1917 Volume 10		
War Diary		01/05/1917	31/05/1917
Heading	War Diary of 4th Cavalry Supply Column From 1st June 1917 To 30th June 1917 Volume 11		
War Diary		01/06/1917	30/06/1917
Heading	War Diary of 4th Cavalry Supply Column From 1st July 1917 To 31st July 1917 Volume 12		
War Diary		01/07/1917	31/07/1917
Heading	War Diary of 4th Cavalry Supply Column From August 1st 1917 To August 31st 1917 Volume 13		
War Diary	Mons En Chaussee	01/08/1917	31/08/1917
Miscellaneous	Headquarters, A.S.C. 4th Cavalry Division.	01/10/1917	01/10/1917
War Diary	Mons En Chaussee	01/09/1917	30/09/1917
Heading	War Diary of 4th Cavalry Supply Column. From 1st October, 1917 To 31st October, 1917 Volume 15		
War Diary		01/10/1917	31/10/1917
Heading	War Diary of 4th Cavalry Supply Column. From 1st November, 1917 To 30th November, 1917 Volume 16		
War Diary		01/11/1917	30/11/1917
Heading	War Diary of 4th Cavalry Supply Column. From 1st December, 1917 To 31st December, 1917 Volume 17		
War Diary		01/12/1917	31/12/1917
Heading	War Diary of 4th Cavalry Supply Column. From 1st January, 1918 To 31st January, 1918 Volume 18		
War Diary		01/01/1918	31/03/1918
Miscellaneous	Statement regarding the loss of Horry W.D. No. 6239 (L.O.) on 29-3-18 Appendix	31/03/1918	31/03/1918
Miscellaneous	D.D.S.T. Fifth Army.	31/03/1918	31/03/1918
Miscellaneous	4th Cav. Sup. Col.	31/03/1918	31/03/1918

WO 95/11258 A1

1917-18
4TH CAVALRY DIVISION

DIVL. SUPPLY COLUMN

JAN 1917-MAR 1918

89 Coy ASC

FROM 1 IND CAV DIV BOX 1173
TO 17 CORPS BOX 949

SERIAL NO. 147.

Confidential

War Diary

of

4TH CAVALRY DIVISIONAL SUPPLY COLUMN.

FROM 1st JANUARY 1917 ~~1916~~ TO 31st JANUARY 1917 ~~1916~~.

Army Form C. 2118.

WAR DIARY
or
INTELLIGENCE SUMMARY.

(Erase heading not required.)

January 1917

Place	Date	Hour	Summary of Events and Information	Remarks and references to Appendices
FRESSENNEVILLE	1/1/17		Raillieul WOINCOURT. Routine	
	2/1/17		Routine	
	3/1/17		The scheme arranged by A.D.M.S. Cavalry Corps to standardise the numbers of laying in each of the Cavalry Divisions under his immediate control to the full into operation. 3 A.D. Divisional lorries were transferred on this account to us in place of 3 Rolleys. Cavalry Clearing Station	
	4/1/17		Routine	
	5/1/17		Routine	
	6/1/17		Routine	
	7/1/17		Routine	

Army Form C. 2118.

WAR DIARY
or
INTELLIGENCE SUMMARY.
(Erase heading not required.)

Instructions regarding War Diaries and Intelligence Summaries are contained in F. S. Regs., Part II. and the Staff Manual respectively. Title pages will be prepared in manuscript.

Place	Date	Hour	Summary of Events and Information	Remarks and references to Appendices
	8/1/17		A.D.S.& T's scheme continued, by transferring from this Column eight C.D. Type Dainless to 5 Cavalry Corps Troops Supply Column	
	9/1/17		Same scheme continued by sending the three Halley lorries from Indenan Cavalry Clearing Station to 2nd Cavalry Supply Column.	
	10/1/17		Routine.	
	11/1/17		Scheme continued by receipt from 3rd Cavalry Supply Column of six 3 ton type Dainless lorries in the place of the C.D. Dainless sent away on 8th inst.	
	12/1/17		Capt. M.y.W. Burton reported as O.C. workshops vice Capt. E.H. Ransom. Authority Q.M.y. O2C. 1366b. of 7.1.17.	
	13/1/17		Routine.	
	14/1/17		Routine	

Army Form C. 2118.

WAR DIARY
or
INTELLIGENCE SUMMARY.

(Erase heading not required.)

Instructions regarding War Diaries and Intelligence Summaries are contained in F. S. Regs., Part II. and the Staff Manual respectively. Title pages will be prepared in manuscript.

Place	Date	Hour	Summary of Events and Information	Remarks and references to Appendices
	15/1/17		Routine	WD/1
	16/1/17		A.D.S.&T.'s column continued by receipt from 5th Cavalry Sup. Col. of G.B. Daurala Lorries.	WD/2
	17/1/17		A.D.S.&T.'s column completed by transferring two Decauville lorries from Field Squadron on 30.12.16 to 5th Cavalry Supply Column for final transfer to the Lines of Communication after inspection by the D. of T. (9 inspection Branch). The nett result of the above has been advantageous to this column as it has reduced the number of lorries for which spare parts have to be carried by the Supply Column, by two. Also it has given an increased mechanical carrying capacity of five and a half tons.	WD/3
	18/1/17		Routine	
	19/1/17		Routine	WD/4

Army Form C. 2118.

WAR DIARY
or
INTELLIGENCE SUMMARY.
(Erase heading not required.)

Instructions regarding War Diaries and Intelligence Summaries are contained in F. S. Regs., Part II. and the Staff Manual respectively. Title pages will be prepared in manuscript.

Place	Date	Hour	Summary of Events and Information	Remarks and references to Appendices
	20/1/17		Routine	Very hard frosts
	21/1/17		"	"
	22/1/17		"	"
	23/1/17		"	"
	24/1/17		"	" Begun to affect the lorries
	25/1/17		"	"
	26/1/17		"	"
	27/1/17		"	"
	28/1/17		"	"

Army Form C.2118.

WAR DIARY
or
INTELLIGENCE SUMMARY.
(*Erase heading not required.*)

Instructions regarding War Diaries and Intelligence Summaries are contained in F. S. Regs., Part II. and the Staff Manual respectively. Title pages will be prepared in manuscript.

Place	Date	Hour	Summary of Events and Information	Remarks and references to Appendices
	29/1/17		Routine	
	30/1/17		Very hard frosts continue	
	31/1/17		" "	

4TH CAVALRY SUPPLY COLUMN
Date 2.2.17.

Major
OC 4th Cavalry Supply Col.

Serial No. 147.

CONFIDENTIAL

WAR DIARY

OF

4TH CAVALRY SUPPLY COLUMN.

From 1.2.17 To 28.2.17

VOLUME 7

H.A. Raymond.
MAJOR.
O.C. 4TH. CAV. SUP. COL.

4TH.
CAVALRY
SUPPLY COLUMN.
No. E72.
Date 1-3-17.

Army Form C. 2118.

WAR DIARY
or
INTELLIGENCE SUMMARY.

4th Cavalry Supply Column

(Erase heading not required.)

Instructions regarding War Diaries and Intelligence Summaries are contained in F. S. Regs., Part II. and the Staff Manual respectively. Title pages will be prepared in manuscript.

Place	Date	Hour	Summary of Events and Information	Remarks and references to Appendices
	FEBRUARY 1917		Railhead WOINCOURT.	
FRESSENNEVILLE	1/2/17		ROUTINE. Very hard frost: motors running rumour casualties is probable set.	WMA
	2/2/17		ROUTINE	WMA
	3/2/17		ROUTINE	WMA
	4/2/17		ROUTINE	WMA
	5/2/17		ROUTINE	WMA
	6/2/17		ROUTINE	WMA
	7/2/17		ROUTINE	WMA

Army Form C. 2118

WAR DIARY

or

INTELLIGENCE SUMMARY.

(Erase heading not required.)

Instructions regarding War Diaries and Intelligence Summaries are contained in F. S. Regs., Part II. and the Staff Manual respectively. Title pages will be prepared in manuscript.

Place	Date	Hour	Summary of Events and Information	Remarks and references to Appendices
	8/2/17		ROUTINE	WW
	9/2/17		ROUTINE	WW
	10/2/17		" "	WW
	11/2/17		Temporary Trans " "	WW
	12/2/17		" "	WW
	13/2/17		" "	WW
	14/2/17		M.T. men enlisted as Drivers but who have been found to be unfit(are) transferred to Auxiliary Roll, and put into remounts, supernumery under authority D of T 1269 d/) 8.2.17. ADST Car Corps P1214 d. 11.2.17. Drivers to be demanded in usual manner to replace them	WW

A 5384 Wt. W4973/M687 750,000 8/16 D. D. & L. Ltd. Forms/C.2118/13.

Army Form C. 2118.

WAR DIARY
or
INTELLIGENCE SUMMARY.

(Erase heading not required.)

Instructions regarding War Diaries and Intelligence Summaries are contained in F. S. Regs., Part II. and the Staff Manual respectively. Title pages will be prepared in manuscript.

Place	Date	Hour	Summary of Events and Information	Remarks and references to Appendices
	15/2/17		Thaw Routine	nil
	16/2/17		Thaw Routine	nil
	17/2/17		Lieut C.F.G. Were evacuated sick, through Lucknow Cas. Fld. Amb. to No. 3. General Hospital at TREPORT.	nil
	18/2/17		Thaw scheme put into operation from 2 P.M. after lorries had loaded at railhead.	nil
	19/2/17		Ditto. Routine. Column did not load at railhead.	nil
	20/2/17		Modified form of Thaw Scheme put into operation. Column continued loading as usual at Railhead, & was made to new refilling points.	nil
	21/2/17		ROUTINE Loads very bad on account of thaw & rain.	nil

Army Form C. 2118.

WAR DIARY
or
INTELLIGENCE SUMMARY.
(Erase heading not required.)

Instructions regarding War Diaries and Intelligence Summaries are contained in F. S. Regs., Part II. and the Staff Manual respectively. Title pages will be prepared in manuscript.

Place	Date	Hour	Summary of Events and Information	Remarks and references to Appendices
	22/2/17		Routine	
	23/2/17		Routine	
	24/2/17		Routine	
	25/2/17		Routine	
	26/2/17		Capt H.W.S. Wright R.A.M.C. reported as Medical Officer to Supply Column. Previous P.O. left divisional area.	
	27/2/17		16 Lorries went on command for Lucerein B'de to 1st Anzac Corps. Troops Supply Column. Lieut J.L. Tucknott in charge. Roads in a very bad state. ROUTINE.	
	28/2/17		Much difficulty experienced in running lorries owing to bad state of the roads after the thaw. ROUTINE	

W.L.Raymond.
MAJOR.
O.C.4TH.CAV.SUP.COL.

Serial No: 147

CONFIDENTIAL
WAR DIARY
OF
4TH CAVALRY SUPPLY COLUMN.

From 1-3-17 To 31-3-17

VOLUME 8

4TH CAVALRY SUPPLY COLUMN.
No...... 16.
Date......

Army Form C. 2118.

WAR DIARY
or
INTELLIGENCE SUMMARY.

(Erase heading not required.)

Instructions regarding War Diaries and Intelligence Summaries are contained in F. S. Regs., Part II. and the Staff Manual respectively. Title pages will be prepared in manuscript.

Place	Date	Hour	Summary of Events and Information	Remarks and references to Appendices
FRESSENNEVILLE	1/3/17		Railroad still WOINCOURT. Routine. Sgt C.T.G. Were evacuated sick to England from No.3. Gen. Hospital	AWM
	2/3/17		Lorries laid up in lines legrad. Supplies carried at railroad by horse transport as under Train releave, on account of bad state of roads, until further orders.	AWM
	3/3/17		Routine.	AWM
	4/3/17		Routine.	AWM
	5/3/17		Routine.	AWM
	6/3/17		Routine.	AWM
	7/3/17		Routine.	AWM

Army Form C. 2118.

WAR DIARY
or
INTELLIGENCE SUMMARY.
(Erase heading not required.)

Instructions regarding War Diaries and Intelligence Summaries are contained in F. S. Regs., Part II. and the Staff Manual respectively. Title pages will be prepared in manuscript.

Place	Date	Hour	Summary of Events and Information	Remarks and references to Appendices
	8/3/17		Recommencement of front. Routine on night of 7-8.	WW
	9/3/17		Routine.	WW
	10/3/17		Lieut C.P. Pearse evacuated sick to No. 3. General Hospital.	WW
	11/3/17		Routine.	WW
	12/3/17		Lucknow Bde Sigs. Sec'tion Lorrie (16) of No.1. Sect. sent up to the Bde at CANAPLES, with this vehicle at CANDAS to join corresponding lorrie of No. 2. Sect. whose arrival Bde. on 27-2-17	WW
	13/3/17		Routine	WW
	14/3/17		Routine	WW

Army Form C. 2118.

WAR DIARY
or
INTELLIGENCE SUMMARY.

(Erase heading not required.)

Instructions regarding War Diaries and Intelligence Summaries are contained in F. S. Regs., Part II. and the Staff Manual respectively. Title pages will be prepared in manuscript.

Place	Date	Hour	Summary of Events and Information	Remarks and references to Appendices
	15/3/17		Routine	MWY
	16/3/17		Advanced workshop under Lieut Rising sent to Lucknow Cell in forward area to CANAPLES.	MWY
	17/3/17		Routine	MWY
	18/3/17		Routine	MWY
	19/3/17		12.30 a.m. Informed that Division would move on 19th. Proceeded to and surplus stores to Dumps. No 1 Sect. moved in our billets, with final rendezvous at CAMBRON at 2.30 P.M. Billeting area of Div. round BUIGNY ST MACLOU.	MWY
	20/3/17		Left FRESSENNEVILLE, passed night at CANAPLES. Railroad POINEDURT.	MWY

Army Form C. 2118.

WAR DIARY
or
INTELLIGENCE SUMMARY.

(Erase heading not required.)

Instructions regarding War Diaries and Intelligence Summaries are contained in F. S. Regs., Part II. and the Staff Manual respectively. Title pages will be prepared in manuscript.

Place	Date	Hour	Summary of Events and Information	Remarks and references to Appendices
	21/3/17		Left CANAPLES 8.30 am. Proceeded to ALBERT via AMIENS. Reached ALBERT. Paraded in BOUZINCOURT Area.	WOR
	22/3/17		Reached ALBERT. Routine.	WOR
	23/3/17		" " Routine	WOR
	24/3/17		" " Routine	WOR
	25/3/17		Reviewed AVELUY Routine	WOR
	26/3/17		" "	WOR
	27/3/17		" "	WOR

A 5834 Wt.W4973/M687 750,000 8/16 D.D.& L.Ltd Forms/C.2118/13.

Army Form C. 2118.

WAR DIARY
or
INTELLIGENCE SUMMARY.
(Erase heading not required.)

Instructions regarding War Diaries and Intelligence Summaries are contained in F. S. Regs., Part II. and the Staff Manual respectively. Title pages will be prepared in manuscript.

Place	Date	Hour	Summary of Events and Information	Remarks and references to Appendices
Railhead still AVELUY	28/3/17		Routine	nil
"	29/3/17		"	nil
"	30/3/17		"	nil
"	31/3/17		"	nil

4TH CAVALRY SUPPLY COLUMN.
No. ....
Date 31.3.17

H.P.Rayxxxxx
MAJOR.
O.C. 4TH. CAV. SUP. COL.

Serial No: 147

CONFIDENTIAL

WAR DIARY

OF

4TH CAVALRY SUPPLY COLUMN

VOLUME 9

From 1st April 1917 To 30th April 1917

W.P. Raymond
MAJOR.
O.C. 4TH CAV. SUP. COL.

Army Form C.2118.

WAR DIARY
or
INTELLIGENCE SUMMARY.
(Erase heading not required.)

Instructions regarding War Diaries and Intelligence Summaries are contained in F. S. Regs., Part II. and the Staff Manual respectively. Title pages will be prepared in manuscript.

Place	Date	Hour	Summary of Events and Information	Remarks and references to Appendices
	APRIL 1st 1914		Railhead AVELUY. Situation on ALBERT – BOUZINCOURT Road. 2/Lieut E.C. Shuter transferred for duty to A.H.T. Coy. Authority ceases 4th Cav. Div. F6. d/31-3-17.	MWW
	2/4/17		Routine.	MWW
	3/4/17		Railhead moved to MIRAUMONT. Loading by M.T. for 1 Brigade & Div. Troops only. Remainder of Lorries am Fifth Army exchange transport as usual.	MWW
	4/4/17		— Routine —	MWW
	5/4/17		" "	MWW
	6/4/17		" " 6 Ford ambulances received from Cav. Corps Troops Supp. Col. Div. Hd Qrs moved to B/HUCOURT.	MWW
	7/4/17		" " 6 Sunbeam ambulances sent from Div. to C.C.T.S. Col. vice 6 Fords above.	MWW

Army Form C. 2118.

WAR DIARY
or
INTELLIGENCE SUMMARY.
(Erase heading not required.)

Instructions regarding War Diaries and Intelligence Summaries are contained in F. S. Regs., Part II. and the Staff Manual respectively. Title pages will be prepared in manuscript.

Place	Date	Hour	Summary of Events and Information	Remarks and references to Appendices
	8/4/17		Routine	WD
	9/4/17		—	WD
	10/4/17		No.1 Sect moved early carrying D.I.S.T. Fifth Army supplies to ACHIET LE GRAND. Three empty to MIRAUMONT railhead to load for Division. Parked between BEHAGNIES and SAPIGNIES. Workshops sent to join Armoured Shop at BIHUCOURT, except one shop left in ALBERT to complete repairs. Temp. 2nd Lieut A.H. MILLS ASC joined for duty from M.T. School of Instruction at C.F.E. Wern. Posted to No.1 Sect. Authy for Enmoyth R.M.G. G.H.Q. 026/15424 d/6.4.17.	WD
	11/4/17		Routine. Workshop turned out of BIHUCOURT and put on BEHAGNIES — SAPIGNIES road. Railhead moved to ACHIET LE GRAND.	WD
	12/4/17		Routine.	WD

A5834 Wt.W4973/M687 750,000 8/16 D.D. & L. Ltd. Forms/C.2118/13.

Army Form C. 2118.

WAR DIARY
or
INTELLIGENCE SUMMARY.
(Erase heading not required.)

Instructions regarding War Diaries and Intelligence Summaries are contained in F. S. Regs., Part II. and the Staff Manual respectively. Title pages will be prepared in manuscript.

Place	Date	Hour	Summary of Events and Information	Remarks and references to Appendices
	13/4/17		No. 1 Sect. rejoined Column. Headquarters at ALBERT. Workshops return from SAPIGNIES to ALBERT.	
	14/4/17		RAILHEAD ALBERT. D.H.Q. MARIEUX.	
	15/4/17		ROUTINE	
	16/4/17		"	
	17/4/17		"	
	18/4/17		"	
	19/4/17		"	
	20/4/17		"	
	21/4/17		"	

WAR DIARY
or
INTELLIGENCE SUMMARY.

(Erase heading not required.)

Army Form C. 2118.

Place	Date	Hour	Summary of Events and Information	Remarks and references to Appendices
	22/4/17		Lieut S.R. waters Smith left Column to be acting B.T.O. Lucknow Bde, vice Capt C.R. Brown who appointed Adjutant 4th A.S.C. in Cav Div. Authority for transfer of Lt Smith Z.117 d. 20-4-17. Routine.	WWJ
	23/4/17		Routine.	WWJ
	24/4/17		Lieut C.R. Reaver rejoined for duty from Hospital.	WWJ
	25/4/17		No.1. Sect moved to MARIEUX in anticipation of railhead moving to BELLE EGLISE on 26th. B.T.O. MAJOR.	WWJ
	26/4/17		Railhead BELLE EGLISE. Headquarters of Column 4 No.1. Sect. parked at MARIEUX. No.2. Section remains at ALBERT. Capt W. SHAW left unit to assume command No. 14 Corps Troops Supply Column. Authority PMG. ASC. 15600	WWJ
	27/4/17		Routine.	WWJ

Army Form C. 2118.

WAR DIARY
or
INTELLIGENCE SUMMARY.
(Erase heading not required.)

Instructions regarding War Diaries and Intelligence Summaries are contained in F. S. Regs., Part II. and the Staff Manual respectively. Title pages will be prepared in manuscript.

Place	Date	Hour	Summary of Events and Information	Remarks and references to Appendices
	28/7/17		Capt. W.H. Sealy reported for duty from 4th Corps Troops Supply Column, posted as O.C. No.1. Sect. vice Capt. W. Shaw.	(illeg)
	29/7/17		2 Lieut J.W. Bridge reported for duty as Supply Officer vice 2 Lieut ___ posted to No.2 Sect.	nil
	30/7/17		Routine.	nil

M.P. Raymond
MAJOR.
O.C. 4TH. CAV. SUP. COL.

Serial No: 147.

CONFIDENTIAL

WAR DIARY

OF

4TH CAVALRY SUPPLY COLUMN

FROM MAY 1ST/17

To MAY 31ST/17

JUNE 30TH/1917.

VOLUME 10.

4TH
CAVALRY
SUPPLY COLUMN.
No. 461
Date 1-6-17

Army Form C. 2118.

WAR DIARY
or
INTELLIGENCE SUMMARY.
(Erase heading not required.)

Place	Date	Hour	Summary of Events and Information	Remarks and references to Appendices
	MAY 1/1917		Railhead still BELLE EGLISE. Column situated :- No 1. Sect. 4 Advanced Dumps at MARIEUX. No 2. Sect between ALBERT and BOUZINCOURT. 15' lorries under Lieut Bedson Attached to Corps Salvage Officer V Corps. stationed at MAILLY-MAILLET.	MM
	2/5/17		Routine	MM
	3/5/17		Routine	MM
	4/5/17		Routine	MM
	5/5/17		Routine	MM
	6/5/17		Routine	MM

Army Form C. 2118.

WAR DIARY
or
INTELLIGENCE SUMMARY.
(Erase heading not required.)

Place	Date	Hour	Summary of Events and Information	Remarks and references to Appendices
Routtin	7/5/17			WAR
	8/5/17		No 2 Sub moved to MARIEUX. Advanced wireless left at ALBERT. Half am of wireless is moved to MARIEUX under W.O.	WAR
Routtin	9/5/17			WAR
	10/5/17		Lorries returned from 1st Anzac Corps and 5th Corps Salvage.	WAR
Rouline	11/5/17			WAR
Rouline	12/5/17			WAR

WAR DIARY or INTELLIGENCE SUMMARY.

Army Form C. 2118.

(Erase heading not required.)

Place	Date	Hour	Summary of Events and Information	Remarks and references to Appendices
	13/3/17		Rouvlin	NWW
	14/3/17		No. 2 Sect. moved to Bde areas to be used on nights 15/16. MEAULTE. TREUX. VILLE sous CORBIE. MERICOURT. AVELUY.	NWW
	15/3/17		No 2 Sect 4 pont wasteralays left MARIEUX 7am & went via ALBERT - BRAY VILLERS CARBONNEL - PERONNE to new Bivouac ar near MESNIL (O.24.d. 40346. Sheet 62c). No 1 Sect loaded at MARIEUX and moved to PROYART via ALBERT and BRAY. (R20.b. Sheet 62D). Col H&R no O.346. (62c)	NWW
	16/3/17		No 1 Sect delivered to Brigades areas named BRAY. No. 2 Sect loaded at new railhead PERONNE - LACHAPPELLETTE. and dumped at PIOSIC. (62c)	NWW
	17/3/17		D.H.Q. ATHIES. Rouvlin	NWW
	18/3/17		Rouvlin	NWW

Army Form C. 2118

WAR DIARY
or
INTELLIGENCE SUMMARY.
(Erase heading not required.)

Place	Date	Hour	Summary of Events and Information	Remarks and references to Appendices
	19/3/17		Routine	MOA
	20/3/17		Routine	MOA
	21/3/17		Routine	MOA
	22/3/17		Column Hd Qrs, Workshops and No 2 Sect moved to MONS EN CHAUSSÉE	MOA
	23/3/17		Iame by lorry to advanced area convened. Refilling point just outside ROISEL on HERVILLY Road.	MOA
	24/3/17		Routine. Delivery to Lucknow Pt to commence at HAMELET.	MOA
	25/3/17		Routine as above.	MOA

Army Form C. 2118.

WAR DIARY
or
INTELLIGENCE SUMMARY.
(Erase heading not required.)

Instructions regarding War Diaries and Intelligence Summaries are contained in F. S. Regs., Part II. and the Staff Manual respectively. Title pages will be prepared in manuscript.

Place	Date	Hour	Summary of Events and Information	Remarks and references to Appendices
	26/5/17		Routine	MAR
	27/5/17		No.1. Section rejoined Column Headquarters at MONS EN CHAUSSÉE. Leaving one lorry and trailer awaiting spares, at PROYART.	MAR
	28/5/17		Routine	MAR
	29/5/17		—	MAR
	30/5/17		—	MAR
	31/5/17		—	MAR

A.H. Raymond
MAJOR.
O.C. 4TH. CAV. SUP. COL.

CONFIDENTIAL

WAR DIARY

OF

4TH CAVALRY SUPPLY COLUMN

From 1st June 1917 To 30th June 1917

VOLUME 11

H.P. Raymond
MAJOR.
O.C. 4TH. CAV. SUP. COL.

4TH CAVALRY SUPPLY COLUMN.
No. 10
Date. 1-7-17

Army Form C. 2118.

WAR DIARY
or
INTELLIGENCE SUMMARY.
(Erase heading not required.)

Instructions regarding War Diaries and Intelligence Summaries are contained in F. S. Regs., Part II. and the Staff Manual respectively. Title pages will be prepared in manuscript.

4TH CAVALRY SUPPLY COLUMN.
No. ....
Date. 1-7-17

Place	Date	Hour	Summary of Events and Information	Remarks and references to Appendices
	JUNE 1917			
	1/6/17		Railhead still PERONNE - LA CHAPELLETTE. Routine.	WD
	2/6/17		Routine.	WD
	3/6/		— " —	WD
	4/6/		— " —	WD
	5/6/		— " —	WD
	6/6/		"B" Sub-unit this detailed working party, joined up at MONS en CHAUSSÉE from PROYART	WD
	7/6/		Routine	WD
	8/6/		Routine	WD
	9/6/		Routine	WD

A5834 Wt.W4973/M687 750,000 8/16 D, D. & L. Ltd. Forms/C.2118/13.

Army Form C. 2118.

WAR DIARY
or
INTELLIGENCE SUMMARY.

(Erase heading not required.)

Instructions regarding War Diaries and Intelligence Summaries are contained in F. S. Regs., Part II and the Staff Manual respectively. Title pages will be prepared in manuscript.

Place	Date	Hour	Summary of Events and Information	Remarks and references to Appendices
	10/6		Routine	
	11/6		Routine	
	12/6		Routine	
	13/6		Routine	
	14/6		Routine	
	15/6		Routine	
	16/6		Routine	
	17/6		Routine	
	18/6		Routine	

WAR DIARY
or
INTELLIGENCE SUMMARY.

(Erase heading not required.)

Army Form C. 2118.

Place	Date	Hour	Summary of Events and Information	Remarks and references to Appendices
	19/6/17		T. 2/Lt. A.H. MILLS evacuated sick to the Base.	AAA
	20/6/17		Routine	AAA
	21/6/17		Routine	AAA
	22/6/17		Routine	AAA
	23/6/17		Routine	AAA
	24/6/17		Routine	AAA
	25/6/17		Routine	AAA

Army Form C. 2118.

WAR DIARY
or
INTELLIGENCE SUMMARY.
(Erase heading not required.)

Place	Date	Hour	Summary of Events and Information	Remarks and references to Appendices
	26/6/17		Routine	W.W.
	27/6/17		The following vehicles of the Column were unrepaired. Sunbeam car 1566. Daimler B. Lorry W.D. No. 7219. L.G.O.C. W.D.No. 3670. L.G.O.C. W.D.No. 3169. all units without chains.	W.W.
	28/6/17		Divisional Ambulances inspected by M.T. Inspection.	W.W.
	29/6/17		No.1. Section 4 ton Workshop left MONS en CHAUSSEE to billet in AMIENS. (Left MONS at 10 am)	W.W.
	30/6/17		Routine	W.W.

MAJOR.
O.C. 4TH. CAV. SUP. COL.

Serial No. 144

CONFIDENTIAL

WAR DIARY

OF

4ᵀᴴ CAVALRY SUPPLY COLUMN

From 1ˢᵀ July 1917 To 31ˢᵀ July 1917

VOLUME 12

W. Maybrul
MAJOR.
O.C. 4TH. CAV. SUP. COL.

4TH CAVALRY SUPPLY COLUMN.
No. 264
Date...............

Army Form C. 2118.

WAR DIARY
or
INTELLIGENCE SUMMARY.
(Erase heading not required.)

4TH CAVALRY SUPPLY COLUMN.
No.... Vol. 12.

Instructions regarding War Diaries and Intelligence Summaries are contained in F.S. Regs., Part II. and the Staff Manual respectively. Title pages will be prepared in manuscript.

Place	Date	Hour	Summary of Events and Information	Remarks and references to Appendices
	JULY 1/7/17 1917		Railhead still PERONNE - LACHAPELETTE. Hd Qrs Column and No. 2 Section situated MONS EN CHAUSSEE. No. 1. Section and detailed Workshop at AMIENS.	WW
	2/7/17			WW
	3/7/17		Received notification (Cav. Corps A/109) That 2nd Lt A.H. MILLS has been evacuated sick to England on 22 June. Casualty shown under following number 23/6. (R/G. O.C. 2/B. R.C.H.	WW
	4/7/17		Routine	WW
	5/7/17		New establishment (No. 5/33) of a Cavalry Supply Column received. Involves reduction of one road officer for Section and also, 4 M.T. Drivers & 1 Batman per section. Total reduction; 2 1st offices, 8 M.T. Drivers, 2 Batmen. (O.E. 381/81 now obsolete.) Orders received for Capt M.W.B. Wright to report to No. 39.	WW

Army Form C. 2118.

WAR DIARY
or
INTELLIGENCE SUMMARY.
(Erase heading not required.)

Instructions regarding War Diaries and Intelligence Summaries are contained in F. S. Regs., Part II. and the Staff Manual respectively. Title pages will be prepared in manuscript.

Place	Date	Hour	Summary of Events and Information	Remarks and references to Appendices
	5/7/17		C.C.S. for duty, is permanently ADMS. 4th Cav. Div. M/3043 d/ 5/7/17. Capt Winget quitted for return address via Irun to U.K.	WW
	6/7/17		Temp/Lieut H.W. FRANK (Q.W.) reports for duty (over Lt A.H. MILLS) from M.T. school of Instruction St OMER, and posted to No 1. Sect. Authority AQ&G (R) AS.E. GHQ 168/31. d 2/7/17. Received notification that "Lt A.H. MILLS was attaché of Exp. Frank August 22/6/17 Daily. QMG.647 AS0/18216/11.	WW
	7/7/17		Routine Following reinforcement during retired Daimlers B. 3 tm W.D.No. 38865 // Daimler LB. 13484 and Daimler C.B. 12351.	WW
	8/7/17		Routine	WW
	9/7/17		The following lorries were inspected, Daimler B. 3 ton W.D.No. 5593 authority ADST Cav. Corp. T504/11/3 d19/4/14. L.G.O.C. W.D. No. 8515, authority ADST " T/504/10/1 d/6/4/14. T/504/11/5 d19/4/14.	WW

Army Form C. 2118.

WAR DIARY
or
INTELLIGENCE SUMMARY.
(Erase heading not required.)

Place	Date	Hour	Summary of Events and Information	Remarks and references to Appendices
Roulers	10/7/17		Routine	[illeg.]
Roulers	11/7/17		Routine	[illeg.]
Roulers	12/7/17		Routine	[illeg.]
	13/7/17		Following lorries received from 5th Aux. Petrol Coy as supplements for those evacuated:- 9 ft winter 7, Daimler 3 ton, W.D. No. 20798. C.B. Daimler, 2 ton (30 cwt nominal) W.D. No. 3671.	[illeg.]
	14/7/17		Routine	[illeg.]

Army Form C. 2118.

WAR DIARY
or
INTELLIGENCE SUMMARY.
(Erase heading not required.)

Instructions regarding War Diaries and Intelligence Summaries are contained in F. S. Regs., Part II. and the Staff Manual respectively. Title pages will be prepared in manuscript.

Place	Date	Hour	Summary of Events and Information	Remarks and references to Appendices
	15/7/17		Routine. Lorry W.D. No. 5685, Daimler B. 3Ton, evacuated to 2nd asc. repair shops under authority A.D.S.T. Cav. Corps. T504/11/3 dated 8-7-17.	WD
	16/7/17		Routine	WD
	17/7/17		"	WD
	18/7/17		"	WD
	19/7/17		"	WD
	20/7/17		"	WD

Army Form C. 2118.

WAR DIARY
or
INTELLIGENCE SUMMARY.
(Erase heading not required.)

Instructions regarding War Diaries and Intelligence Summaries are contained in F. S. Regs., Part II. and the Staff Manual respectively. Title pages will be prepared in manuscript.

Place	Date	Hour	Summary of Events and Information	Remarks and references to Appendices
	21/7/17		Private B. Long 3 Coy W.D. No. 2760 arrived from 15 Res. Petrol Coy. as replacement of the own evacuated on 15/7.	WJH
	22/7/17		Routine	WJH
	23/7/17		Routine	WJH
	24/7/17		1st Lieut. F.H. Hunt. United States Medical Corps (Reserve) joined as M.O. 15 Column.	WJH
	25/7/17		Wolseley car W.D. No. 554 allotted to D.A.D.O.S. D.H.Q. transferred to 3rd A.S.C. Repair Shop. STOMER. Covered chassis Dodge A.D.S.T. Cars. Comn.T/505/M/4 dated 23-7-17	WJH

Army Form C. 2118.

WAR DIARY
or
INTELLIGENCE SUMMARY.
(Erase heading not required.)

Instructions regarding War Diaries and Intelligence Summaries are contained in F. S. Regs., Part II. and the Staff Manual respectively. Title pages will be prepared in manuscript.

Place	Date	Hour	Summary of Events and Information	Remarks and references to Appendices
	26/7/17		Daimler B. (Steam) lorry evacuated with cracked chassis to 2nd ASC Repair Shop, ROUEN. W.D. No. of lorry 5684. Authy A.D.S.T. Corps T/504/11/5 dated 23/7/17.	MM
	27/7/17		Routine	MM
	28/7/17		Routine	MM
	29/7/17		Routine. Maxwell car W.D. No. 29838 arrived from 5th Aux. Petrol Coy in replacement of 554 Wolseley wrecked. Allotted to 29838 4th Cav.	MM
	30/7/17		Maxwell car 29838 handed over to Camp Commandant.	MM
	31/7/17		Routine	MM

2353 Wt. W2544/1454 700,000 5/15 D. D. & L. A.D.S.S./Forms/C. 2118.

M.M. Raymond
MAJOR.
O.C. 4TH CAV. SUP. COL.

Serial No: 144.

CONFIDENTIAL.

WAR DIARY

OF

4TH CAVALRY SUPPLY COLUMN

VOLUME 13

From August 1st 1917 — To August 31st 1917

H.P. Raymond
MAJOR.
O.C. 4TH CAVALRY SUP. COL.

WAR DIARY
or
INTELLIGENCE SUMMARY.

Army Form C. 2118.

4TH CAVALRY SUPPLY COLUMN.
No. Vol. 13

Place	Date	Hour	Summary of Events and Information	Remarks and references to Appendices
MONS EN CHAUSSÉE	AUGUST 1917 1.		Railhead altd PERONNE - LACHAPELLETTE (since 16th d/ay). Y. Daimler Lorry W.D.NO. 16263 received from 5th Aux. Petrol Coy in replacement of lorry evacuated on 26-7-17.	WWW
	2.		Routine	WWW
	3.		Routine	WWW
	4.		No.1. Section returned from detachment at AMIENS, and rejoined the Column at MONS EN CHAUSSÉE. Routine.	WWW
	5.		Routine	WWW
	6.		Seventy two Lorries under Capt Seely employed in moving Dismounted Brigade to EPEHY. Daimler D. Lorry W.D. NO. 5620 evacuated to 2nd ASC Repair Shops.	WWW

Army Form C. 2118.

WAR DIARY
or
INTELLIGENCE SUMMARY.
(Erase heading not required.)

Instructions regarding War Diaries and Intelligence Summaries are contained in F. S. Regs., Part II. and the Staff Manual respectively. Title pages will be prepared in manuscript.

Place	Date	Hour	Summary of Events and Information	Remarks and references to Appendices
	7		Routine	
	8		Routine	
	9		Temp. 2/Lieut T. R. RIDPATH left the column to (Rueplyo to establishment) to report to O.C. "I" corps Siege Park for duty with 293rd Siege Battery, Authority A.Q.M.G. (P) A.S.C. G.H.Q. 17047 dated 29/7/19.	
	10		Routine	
	11		acting W.O. class I (M53880 Sergt (a/W.S.M) COPE AT reverted to permanent rank sergeant for inefficiency	
	12		Above named individual sent to the Base (No.1. B.M.T.D.) P&V.E.N. Y. Daiular lorry 26588 received from 5th Aux. Petrol Coy to replace the one evacuated on 8th inst.	
	13		Routine	

Army Form C. 2118.

WAR DIARY
or
INTELLIGENCE SUMMARY.
(Erase heading not required.)

Instructions regarding War Diaries and Intelligence Summaries are contained in F. S. Regs., Part II. and the Staff Manual respectively. Title pages will be prepared in manuscript.

Place	Date	Hour	Summary of Events and Information	Remarks and references to Appendices
	14		Routine	MM
	15		Commencing with No. 1. Section, on this date, the two Sections loading on alternate days.	MM
	16		Routine	MM
	17		Major Raymond proceeded on leave to U.K.	MM
	18		Capt. W. H. Dapper R.A.M.C. reported & was taken on the strength. Lieut. F. H. Hunt U.S.M.C. Dismissed to Southwick Camp D.Y.	MM
	18		Received notification from Q.M.G. B.H.Q. that Capt. N.C.W. Bointon was returned at home for duty, he being on leave at the time.	MM
	18		Lieut J.W.C. Barnett left the Column (Shoeburn) to establishment) to report to O.C. 15th Corps Troops Sup Col for duty Authority Q.M.G. A.S.C. M270 A 27.8.17.	MM
	19		M2/53116 Pte (a/C.Q.M.S.) Richardson H.R. reverted to his permanent rank of Private for "misconduct"	MM
	20		Routine.	MM

Army Form C. 2118.

WAR DIARY
or
INTELLIGENCE SUMMARY.
(Erase heading not required.)

Instructions regarding War Diaries and Intelligence Summaries are contained in F.S. Regs., Part II. and the Staff Manual respectively. Title pages will be prepared in manuscript.

Place	Date	Hour	Summary of Events and Information	Remarks and references to Appendices
	21		Routine	
	22		Captain J S Crawford returned for duty from the 31 Div Sul C.R.	
	23		Routine	
	24		Routine	
	25		26 men transferred to No 1 B and M.T. Depot surplus to establishment auth A.D.S.&T. P1258/A/22.8.17	
	26		Routine	
	27		27 men transferred to No 1 B M.T. Depot Surplus to establishment Bringing the total up to 53 men Authorized Deduction auth A.D.&T. P1258/A/22.8.17 Two L.O.R. lorries No's W.D. 3079 - 3863 evacuated to No 2 A.S.C Rebais Shop ROUEN auth A.D.&T. Cert Cod. T 504/A/6.A/23.8.17	
	28		Routine	

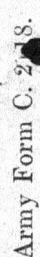

Army Form C.2118.

WAR DIARY
or
INTELLIGENCE SUMMARY.

(Erase heading not required.)

Instructions regarding War Diaries and Intelligence Summaries are contained in F. S. Regs., Part II. and the Staff Manual respectively. Title pages will be prepared in manuscript.

Place	Date	Hour	Summary of Events and Information	Remarks and references to Appendices
	29	Routine		WW
	30	Routine		WW
	31	Routine		WW

A.P. Raymond
MAJOR.
O.C. 4TH CAVALRY SUP. COL.

CONFIDENTIAL.

Headquarters, A.S.C.

4th Cavalry Division.

　　　Herewith War Diary of 4th Cavalry Supply Column Volume 14 from 1st September, 1917, to 30th September, 1917.

1-10-17.

H P Raymaul
Major.
O.C. 4th Cav.Sup.Col.

Army Form C. 2118.

SEPTEMBER 1917
Vol. XIV

4TH CAVALRY SUPPLY COLUMN.

WAR DIARY
or
INTELLIGENCE SUMMARY.
(Erase heading not required.)

Instructions regarding War Diaries and Intelligence Summaries are contained in F. S. Regs., Part II. and the Staff Manual respectively. Title pages will be prepared in manuscript.

Place	Date	Hour	Summary of Events and Information	Remarks and references to Appendices
MONS EN CHAUSSÉE	1/9/17		Railhead still PERONNE – LACHAPELETTE. Routine.	APR.
	2/9/17		The Column Medical Officer, Capt. W.H. RAYNER, R.A.M.C. left the Column to report to on 4th Reserve Park for duty, The Column remaining under his medical charge. Routine.	WPR
	3/9/17		Routine.	WPR
	4/9/17		Routine.	WPR
	5/9/17		Routine.	WPR
	6/9/17		Routine.	WPR

Army Form C. 2118.

WAR DIARY
or
INTELLIGENCE SUMMARY.
(Erase heading not required.)

Instructions regarding War Diaries and Intelligence Summaries are contained in F. S. Regs., Part II. and the Staff Manual respectively. Title pages will be prepared in manuscript.

Place	Date	Hour	Summary of Events and Information	Remarks and references to Appendices
	7/9/17		Routine	MWF
	8/9/17		Routine	MWF
	9/9/17		Routine	MWF
	10/9/17		Routine	MWF
	11/9/17		L.G.O.C. Lorry W.D. No. 2280 reported from 5th Aux. Pet. Coy. as evacuated on 29.7.17. The second replacement is shown on one of those evacuated. To report from 4th Cav. Sanitary Section under A.D.S.T.C.C. T.S.O+/12/6 26/9/17 A.D.57 C.C replacement in due course but so far has not arrived.	MWF
	12/9/17		Routine	MWF

Army Form C. 2118.

WAR DIARY
or
INTELLIGENCE SUMMARY.
(Erase heading not required.)

Place	Date	Hour	Summary of Events and Information	Remarks and references to Appendices
	13/9/17		1 Car and 2 cycles transferred as under, on account of authorized deduction under ADSTn No. T/895. d/10-9-17 Maxwell Car W.D. 44294 to 2nd Army Troops Supply Column, RENESOURE. Douglas bycles Frame Nos. 33964 and 21251 to D.D.T. Southern, ABBEVILLE. Ford bore car to Sanitary Section reported from C.C.T.S.C.	MWR
	14/9/17		Ford boxcar (above) detailed with Sup. Col. pending further instructions, under order from Hd. Qrs. A.S.C. 4th Cav.	MWR
	15/9/17		Routine	MWR
	16/9/17		20 lorries, under 2/Lt Benjamin, reported for temporary duty from 2nd Cav. Sup. Col.	MWR
	17/9/17		20 lorries, under 2/Lt Bowers, reported for temporary duty from 3rd Cav. Sup. Col.	MWR

Army Form C. 2118.

WAR DIARY
or
INTELLIGENCE SUMMARY.
(Erase heading not required.)

Instructions regarding War Diaries and Intelligence Summaries are contained in F. S. Regs., Part II. and the Staff Manual respectively. Title pages will be prepared in manuscript.

Place	Date	Hour	Summary of Events and Information	Remarks and references to Appendices
PARIS.	18/9/17		Lieut A. M Beatson left the column for duty with 1st A.S.C. Repair Shop, authority Q.M.G. A.S.C. 17766 2/11/9/17.	MWA
	19/9/17		Routine.	MWA
	20/9/17		Routine. Transport of Stabling, hutting est for the other Cavalry Divisions, from BRIE STATION to new Divisional areas, commenced.	MWA
	21/9/17		Routine.	MWA
	22/9/17		Routine.	MWA
	23/9/17		Routine.	MWA

WAR DIARY
or
INTELLIGENCE SUMMARY.

(Erase heading not required.)

Army Form C. 2118.

Place	Date	Hour	Summary of Events and Information	Remarks and references to Appendices
Routine	24/9/17			WAR
Routine	25/9/17			WAR
	26/9/17		Establishment of Lorries reduced by 20 (10 fr Section). ADST. Cav. Corps M/15800/2 . 3.9.17. and 23.9.17.	WAR
	27/9/17		20 Lorries left under above authority to report as follows:- 3 to S.M.T.O. VIII Corps. 7 to SMTO IX Corps. 10 to S.M.T.O. X Corps. Temp. 2 Lieut J.C. Andrews reported for duty, vice Lieut A.M. Beaton, (transferred to Paris 18th earlier)	WAR
Routine	28/9/17			WAR
Routine	29/9/17			WAR
Routine	30/9/17			WAR

MRayHenry MAJOR.
O.C. 4TH CAVALRY SUP. COL.

CONFIDENTIAL

WAR DIARY.

of

4th CAVALRY SUPPLY COLUMN.

From   1st October, 1917.   To   31st October, 1917.

Volume 15.

(147.)

| 4TH CAVALRY SUPPLY COLUMN. |
| No.... 627. |

H.P. Raymond
MAJOR.
O.C. 4TH CAVALRY SUP. COL.

Army Form C. 2118.

OCTOBER 1917.

VOL. XV

4TH CAVALRY SUPPLY COLUMN.

WAR DIARY
or
INTELLIGENCE SUMMARY.

(Erase heading not required.)

Place	Date	Hour	Summary of Events and Information	Remarks and references to Appendices
	1/10/17		Column still situated at MONS EN CHAUSSEE. Sheet 62C. P.27.C.4.9. Railhead still PERONNE LACHAPELETTE.	AWR
Rancourt	2/10/17			AWR
Rancourt	3/10/17			AWR
	4/10/17		The 21 Lorries attached from each of 2nd & 3rd Cav. Divns, returned to their respective units between 11 and 12 midnight 4/5.10	AWR
Rancourt	5&6/10/17			AWR
Rancourt	7/10/17			AWR
	8/10/17		L.C.O.O. Lorry W.D. No. 8384 received from 4th Cav. Sanitary Section, to transport. Authority A.D.S.T. Cav. Corps T504/12/5 21/5-/9/17.	AWR

2353 Wt. W2544/1454 700,000 5/15 D. D. & L. A.D.S.S./Forms/C. 2118.

Army Form C. 2118.

WAR DIARY
or
INTELLIGENCE SUMMARY.
(Erase heading not required.)

Instructions regarding War Diaries and Intelligence Summaries are contained in F. S. Regs., Part II. and the Staff Manual respectively. Title pages will be prepared in manuscript.

Place	Date	Hour	Summary of Events and Information	Remarks and references to Appendices
	9/10/17		Routine	[initials]
	10/10/17		Routine	[initials]
	11/10/17		Routine	[initials]
	12/10/17		Routine	[initials]
	13/10/17		Routine	[initials]
	14/10/17		Routine	[initials]
	15/10/17		Routine	[initials]

Army Form C. 2118.

WAR DIARY
or
INTELLIGENCE SUMMARY.
(Erase heading not required.)

Instructions regarding War Diaries and Intelligence Summaries are contained in F. S. Regs., Part II. and the Staff Manual respectively. Title pages will be prepared in manuscript.

Place	Date	Hour	Summary of Events and Information	Remarks and references to Appendices
	16/10/17		Routine	W.D.R.
	17/10/17		Routine	W.D.R.
	18/10/17		Routine	W.D.R.
	19/10/17		Routine	W.D.R.
	20/10/17		Routine	W.D.R.
	21/10/17		Routine	W.D.R.
	22/10/17		Routine. 30 lorries reported drawn 2nd Car Supply Col. for hutting & fuelwood in ESTRÉES EN CHAUSSÉE. These lorries only carried the column iron as far as detail is concerned, their lorries being detailed by their unit.	W.D.R.

Army Form C. 2118.

WAR DIARY
or
INTELLIGENCE SUMMARY.
(Erase heading not required.)

Instructions regarding War Diaries and Intelligence Summaries are contained in F. S. Regs., Part II. and the Staff Manual respectively. Title pages will be prepared in manuscript.

Place	Date	Hour	Summary of Events and Information	Remarks and references to Appendices
	23/10/17		Routine	
	24/10/17		Routine	
	25/10/17		Routine	
	26/10/17		Routine	
	27/10/17		3.0 Lorries reported from 3rd Cav. Sup. Col. for Hutting unloaded. Paraded at LE-MESNIL. attached to 4 in Cav. Sup. Col. for "Details" only.	
	28/10/17		Routine	

Army Form C. 2118.

WAR DIARY
or,
INTELLIGENCE SUMMARY.
(Erase heading not required.)

Instructions regarding War Diaries and Intelligence Summaries are contained in F. S. Regs., Part II. and the Staff Manual respectively. Title pages will be prepared in manuscript.

Place	Date	Hour	Summary of Events and Information	Remarks and references to Appendices
Routine	29/10/17		T/2 Lieut H.W. FRANK admitted sick to No. 55 C.C.S.	MPR
Routine	30/10/17			MPR
Routine	31/10/17			MPR

M.P.Reynard
MAJOR.
O.C. 4TH CAVALRY SUP. COL.

CONFIDENTIAL.

WAR DIARY.

of

4th CAVALRY SUPPLY COLUMN.

From 1st November, 1917.   To 30th November, 1917.

Volume 16.

(147.)

4TH CAVALRY SUPPLY COLUMN.
No. 968
Date.

H.P. Raymond
MAJOR.
O.C. 4TH CAVALRY SUP. COL.

Army Form C. 2118.

1917.
Vol. XVI NOVEMBER.

4TH CAVALRY SUPPLY COLUMN.

WAR DIARY
or
INTELLIGENCE SUMMARY.
(Erase heading not required.)

Instructions regarding War Diaries and Intelligence Summaries are contained in F. S. Regs., Part II. and the Staff Manual respectively. Title pages will be prepared in manuscript.

Place	Date	Hour	Summary of Events and Information	Remarks and references to Appendices
	Nov.1.		Column still situated at MONS-EN-CHAUSSÉE. Sheet 62 C. P 27 C. 4.4. since May 22nd 1917. Railhead still PERONNE LA CHAPELLETTE, since MAY.16.1917.	WWR
	2		Routine	WWR
	3		Routine	WWR
	4		Routine	WWR
	5		Routine	WWR
	6		Routine	WWR
	7		Routine	WWR
	8		Routine	WWR
	9		Routine	WWR

Army Form C. 2118.

WAR DIARY
or
INTELLIGENCE SUMMARY.
(Erase heading not required.)

Instructions regarding War Diaries and Intelligence Summaries are contained in F.S. Regs., Part II and the Staff Manual respectively. Title pages will be prepared in manuscript.

Place	Date	Hour	Summary of Events and Information	Remarks and references to Appendices
	10		Routine	
	11		Routine	
	12		Routine	
	13		Routine	
	14		Statement from 2nd Cav. Supp. Col. regarding their visit from ESTREES. Routine	
	15		Routine	
	16		Routine	
	17		Routine	
	18		Routine. Recommenced normal method of double echelon loading, holding one day's rations outrigger on two lorries.	
	19		Routine	
	20		Column left MONS en CHAUSSEE at 4 PM to new parking ground at RANCOURT Sheet 62 c. C.1.C.3.2.	
	21		Railroad arranged from PERONNE (LACHAPELLETTE) to YTRES. 1 and 15 to arrive at ATHIES. Remainder of Division on forward communications cars at FINS.	

2353 Wt W2544/1454 700,000 5/15 D.D. & L. A.D.S.S./Forms/C. 2118.

Army Form C. 2118.

WAR DIARY
or
INTELLIGENCE SUMMARY.
(Erase heading not required.)

Instructions regarding War Diaries and Intelligence Summaries are contained in F.S. Regs., Part II. and the Staff Manual respectively. Title pages will be prepared in manuscript.

Place	Date	Hour	Summary of Events and Information	Remarks and references to Appendices
	22		Loaded at YTRES. Moved at ATHIES and in forward concentration area at FINS.	MWW
	23		Loaded at YTRES. Both Sections moved in original billets in ATHIES Divisional area. ATHIES moved down to original billets at MONG EN CHAUSSEE.	MWW
	24		Railhead BRIE. No issue	MWW
	25		Railhead BRIE. One issue to Division in Boise Area (ATHIES-ETC)	MWW
	26		" " "	MWW
	27		Capt T.S. Crawford (O o/c workshops) left to report to O.C. "L" Sup. Col. for duty. Capt. J.A. Galbraith reported from "L" Sup. Col. for duty as O o/c Workshops. Authority QMG GHQ wire No. Q.P.1844 d 25/11/14	MWW

2353 Wt. W2544/1454 700,000 5/15 D.D. & L.   A.D.S.S./Forms/C. 2118.

Army Form C. 2118.

WAR DIARY
or
INTELLIGENCE SUMMARY.
(Erase heading not required.)

Instructions regarding War Diaries and Intelligence Summaries are contained in F.S. Regs., Part II. and the Staff Manual respectively. Title pages will be prepared in manuscript.

Place	Date	Hour	Summary of Events and Information	Remarks and references to Appendices
Routine	28			
Routine	29			
	30		Railhead changed from BRIE to PERONNE LACHAPELLETTE. Rations drawn 30th by armed escort, picked up again in transit. Division counterattacking again. One lorry sent in command to 3rd Army dump. ALBERT.	

M.P. Raynard
MAJOR.
O.C. 4TH CAVALRY SUP. COL.

CONFIDENTIAL.

WAR DIARY.

of

4th CAVALRY SUPPLY COLUMN.

From 1st December, 1917.   To 31st December, 1917.

Volume 17.

H.A. Raynard MAJOR.
O.C. 4TH CAVALRY SUP. COL.

Army Form C. 2118.

WAR DIARY
or
INTELLIGENCE SUMMARY.
(Erase heading not required.)

4TH CAVALRY SUPPLY COLUMN. VOL. XVII. DECEMBER 1917

Place	Date	Hour	Summary of Events and Information	Remarks and references to Appendices
DECEMBER	1ST		Railhead PERONNE LACHAPELLETTE. Column parked at MONS EN CHAUSSÉE. (Sheet 62c 1/40000. P.27.C.) Column moved at 3 P.M. to new billets at PROYART.	WWW
	2nd		Railhead LA FLAQUE. Lieut C.P. Reeve sent up to LOUVAISNES to take up Supply Officer i/c forward dump. Lt. J.L. TREDEAFT admitted to hospital. 4 degrees frost.	WWW
	3rd		Lieut C.P. Reeve returned 1.45 a.m. Routine. 4 Degrees frost	WWW
	4		Routine. 9 degrees frost	WWW
	5		GOC Army W.D. No. 6247 transmits under authority ADST Cav Corps T.S.O.4./15/3 d/2.12.17. Divnl Army W.D. No. 3788 (C.D.) received from Lucknow C.C.S. on reduction of their establishment, authority ADST Cav Corps T.919 d/1/12/17	WWW

Army Form C. 2118.

WAR DIARY
or
INTELLIGENCE SUMMARY.
(Erase heading not required.)

Place	Date	Hour	Summary of Events and Information	Remarks and references to Appendices
	6		Routine. Entire day lay delivered to 9 divisions.	MWS
×	7.		Railhead moved to PERONNE LACHAPELETTE. Column moved to ETERPIGNY – VILLERS CARBONNEL road.	MWS
	8		Routine.	MWS
×	9		No issue by M.T. owing to Thaw Scheme.	MWS
×	10		No issue by MT owing to Thaw Scheme.	MWS
	11		Routine. Issue iron.	MWS
×	12		Took over 4th Cav. Divin. Park (less 79 MT by) and absorbed it into the Supply Column, showing Divin Park Special Establishment as an Authorized Addition. Took over :- Capt A.R. Howard ASC Veterinary Officer, "Lieut R.B. Cooker ASC, "Lieut J.S. Shiery R.F.A. (ammunition officer). 2D RHA details, 36 ASC details, 33 lorries including 1 Workshop and one store, 2 cars, 8 motor cycles. Authority for transfer ADST Cav. Corps M/1533 9.12.17	MWS

Army Form C. 2118.

WAR DIARY
or
INTELLIGENCE SUMMARY.
(Erase heading not required.)

Instructions regarding War Diaries and Intelligence Summaries are contained in F. S. Regs., Part II. and the Staff Manual respectively. Title pages will be prepared in manuscript.

Place	Date	Hour	Summary of Events and Information	Remarks and references to Appendices
			To intimate an Ammunition Section under to Supply Column and to remain detached with no Cav. Corps Ammunition Park at ESTREES for purposes of transport detail only.	WM
	13		L.Cor. Lowry 3057 received from Cav. Corps Troops Supply Column to replace 6249 evacuated on 5/12/17. Temp. a/dr. H.W. Franks admitted to Hospital (at AMIENS). Ammunition — 12 lorries to MONTIGNY DUMP units 1525 N.X. and 1919 N.	WM
	14		Routine	MPR
	15		14 lorries reported from 1st Cav. Sup. Col. to be attached to feeding 7th R.H.A. Bde.	WM
	16		L.Cor. Lowry W.D. No. 2638 evacuated. Authy:- A79T Cas. Corps T/504/16/4. Replaced by C.T. Rainsler 3788 received from Lieutenant C.C.S. on 5/12/17.	WM

Army Form C. 2118.

WAR DIARY
or
INTELLIGENCE SUMMARY.

(Erase heading not required.)

Instructions regarding War Diaries and Intelligence Summaries are contained in F. S. Regs., Part II. and the Staff Manual respectively. Title pages will be prepared in manuscript.

Place	Date	Hour	Summary of Events and Information	Remarks and references to Appendices
	17	X	T/Lieut J.F.B. Aahton admitted to Hospital. Heavy snow during night 16/17. Much dislocation of Mechanical Transport Traffic.	
	18		Rouen. Train 12 hours late, consequently no news that date.	
	19		Rouen. Double issue. 16 degrees frost during night 18/19.	
	20		22 degrees frost night 19/20. Column moved from ETERPIGNY to MONS EN CHAUSSÉE, mailvans atts LACHAPELLETTE.	
	21		Capt W. H. Sealy admitted to Hospital and evacuated. No. 1. Sect taken over by 2 Lt J. E. Andrews (Subaltern No. 2. Sect.)	
	22		Routine	
	23	X	T/2 Lieut S.C.E. Fielder attached for temporary duty from Hd Qrs ASC during shortage of officers.	
	24		Routine	

WAR DIARY
or
INTELLIGENCE SUMMARY.

(Erase heading not required.)

Army Form C. 2118.

Place	Date	Hour	Summary of Events and Information	Remarks and references to Appendices
	25		Ascertained that Lieut J.S. Mann 5 Bty. R.F.A. (Ammn. Sect.) was admitted to Hospital on 20th. Have not seen him.	
	26		Routine. Frost resumed.	
	27		Routine	
	28		Routine	
	29		Routine	
	30		Routine	
	31		Routine	

M.P. Raybould
MAJOR.
O.C. 4TH CAVALRY SUP. COL.

CONFIDENTIAL.

WAR DIARY.

of

4th CAVALRY SUPPLY COLUMN.

From 1st January, 1918.   To 31st January, 1918.

Volume 18.

W.P. Raynard
MAJOR.
O.C. 4TH CAVALRY SUP. COL.

Army Form C. 2118.

4TH CAVALRY SUPPLY COLUMN.
No. VOL. 1B

WAR DIARY
or
INTELLIGENCE SUMMARY.
(Erase heading not required.)

JANUARY 1918

Place	Date	Hour	Summary of Events and Information	Remarks and references to Appendices
	JAN. 1918.	1st	Column situated as follows:- Hd Qrs, Workshops, No Supply Section at MONS-EN-CHAUSSEE; Ammunition Section at ESTREES; Railhead PERONNE-LACHAPELLETTE.	seen
		2nd	2 Lieut H.W. Frank rejoined for duty from Hospital.	seen
		3.	Routine	seen
		4.	Routine	seen
		5.	Routine	seen
		6.	Capt J.A. GALBRAITH ASC. O.i/c Workshops transferred to 1st Base M.T. Depot as unfit medically for duty in forward area. Authority Cav. Corps A 5502 d/4.1.18. HdQrs 4th Cav. Divs. B158 d/5.1.18. Lieut J.S. Shiny struck off - transferred to England - sick, on 24/2/17. Cav. Corps A.109. d 2/1/18. "Lt S.E.G. Fielden sent to Peronne for course from 7th to 9th at Fifth Army School of Sanitation.	seen
		7	Routine. THAW SCHEME came into force at 3 P.M. " " " " cancelled at 7.30 P.M.	seen

Army Form C. 2118.

WAR DIARY
or
INTELLIGENCE SUMMARY.
(Erase heading not required.)

Instructions regarding War Diaries and Intelligence Summaries are contained in F. S. Regs., Part II. and the Staff Manual respectively. Title pages will be prepared in manuscript.

Place	Date	Hour	Summary of Events and Information	Remarks and references to Appendices
Rantin	8			nell
Rantin	9			nell
	10		Temp. Lieut. J.F.B Aselin returned to duty from Hospital via 1st Base M.T. Depot. Lt. Fields returned from 5th Army Sanitation course.	nell
	11		Lt S.C.E. Fields posted to A.H.T. Coy & Cas. Div. for duty. Thaw Scheme came into force from 12 midnight.	nell
	12		First day of Thaw, no lorries moved at all.	nell
	13		Second day of Thaw, no lorries moved.	nell
	14		Thaw Scheme OFF. Supply train closed as usual by M.T. also Re. two days dumped at railhead on 12th and 13th.	nell
Rantin	15		Thaw Scheme came into force at 6 P.M.	nell
	16		Thaw Scheme in force. No lorries employed.	nell
	17		Thaw Scheme in force. No lorries employed.	nell

WAR DIARY

or

INTELLIGENCE SUMMARY.

(*Erase heading not required.*)

Army Form C. 2118.

Instructions regarding War Diaries and Intelligence Summaries are contained in F. S. Regs., Part II. and the Staff Manual respectively. Title pages will be prepared in manuscript.

Place	Date	Hour	Summary of Events and Information	Remarks and references to Appendices
	18		Rail Scheme in force states (3rd day) was being reemployed.	WD1
	19		Rail Scheme in force, train being cleared entirely by Horse Transport to Brigade dumps.	WD2
X	20		Rail Scheme in force, same programme reported to an 19th except that 15 three ton and 7 newly cast-downs were turned out at 11am to draw coal and wood from railhead to Brigade.	WD3
	21		Rail Scheme in later units 6 P.M. Only 5' lorries out & for wood from Railhead to Brigades.	WD3
X	22		Rail Scheme off. Drawings from railhead resumed by M.T., but Set. loading off train. Item other off dump. Ammunition Section moved from ESTREES to ETERPIGNY. (Shutzé) O.14.d.3.8.	WD4
	23		One day loaded by MT off the train and one day off the dump. Intelligence P. BRUGIERE transferred to 3rd Cavalry Division.	

Army Form C. 2118.

WAR DIARY
or
INTELLIGENCE SUMMARY:
(Erase heading not required.)

Instructions regarding War Diaries and Intelligence Summaries are contained in F. S. Regs., Part II. and the Staff Manual respectively. Title pages will be prepared in manuscript.

Place	Date	Hour	Summary of Events and Information	Remarks and references to Appendices
	24		One day loaded by M.T. & H train and one day by H train	H
	25		Whole of supplies drawn from train by M.T.	H
	26		Lieutenant M.O. Glos refunded transferred from No. 10 shoeing C.S.	W.O.S
	27		Routine	W.O.Y
	28		—	W.O.Y
X	29		Transferred 26 Albion lorries, 1 Daimler Store Lorry, 53 drivers from Ammunition Section to 1st Cav. Ammn. Park on authority ADST Cav Corps S/62 dated 27.1.18. Lt J.L. Trevenef returned to duty.	W.W
X	30		Lieut J. Laugher R.F.A. reported for duty as artillery officer under Ammunition Sect. (A.G. 2157/419(b)) dated 27.1.18.	W.Y
	31		Routine.	W.W

4TH CAVALRY SUPPLY COLUMN.
No......

H.P. Pughead
MAJOR.
O.C. 4TH CAVALRY SUP. COL.

WAR DIARY or **INTELLIGENCE SUMMARY.**

(Erase heading not required.)

Army Form C. 2118

VOL. 20.

MARCH 1918

4TH CAVALRY SUPPLY COLUMN.

142

Place	Date	Hour	Summary of Events and Information	Remarks and references to Appendices
	1/3/18		Railhead SALEUX. Column pulled in SALEUX. OC on leave. Capt. W.H. SEARY takes over command.	W.S.
	2/3/18		2/Lt J.S. ANDREW + party of 26 ORs detached under 4th Cav Div QA 758 d/1/3/18 to 1st Cav Sup Col at BOIRE.	WHS
	3/3/18		Routine	W.S.
	4/3/18		Routine	W.S.
	5/3/18		Routine	W.S.
	6/3/18		Railhead moves to LONGPRÉ. 2/Lt HORTON sent in sick. Bugler PETE admitted to Hosp Blackburn. J.O.C. a.a.a. Forward application for F.G.C.M. a Pte Blackburn.	W.S.
	7/3/18		ROUTINE	W.S.
	8/3/18		ROUTINE	W.S.
	9/3/18		Three men proceed on 14 days leave. E Dau Coy WD No 2848 hand over near POIX through sleeping trouble.	W.S.

Army Form C. 2118.

WAR DIARY
or
INTELLIGENCE SUMMARY.
(Erase heading not required.)

MARCH 1918

Instructions regarding War Diaries and Intelligence Summaries are contained in F. S. Regs., Part II. and the Staff Manual respectively. Title pages will be prepared in manuscript.

Place	Date	Hour	Summary of Events and Information	Remarks and references to Appendices
	10/3/18		ROUTINE	WWS
	11.3.18		ROUTINE	WWS
	12.3.18		Routine	WWS
	13.3.18		Obtain receipt from O.C. A.R.E. 5th Car Du Parte for following M.T. Vehicles proceeding overseas which have been handed over to him. 9 cars. 2 Boxcars 23 Ambulances 1 Solo Car Combination 12 m/cycles. Car sent to Purchasing Officer Cav Corps for one week under orders of A.D.S.T. Cav Corps.	WWS
	14.3.18		ROUTINE	WWS
	15.3.18		Receive instructions from O.C. A.S.C. to transfer all M.T. vehicles in charge, except our own, to 5th Cav Sup Col MDST. Cav Corps came down to see about cars whilst me. Capt. Major M.P. Reynaud 25th yet returned from leave.	WWS
	16.3.18		Transfer all M.T. Vehicles of 4th Cav Div to 5th Car Sup Col except 2 m/cycles. 4th Car Reserve Park F.O.8.en Dumpeter sent to Boves with M.T. Carton orders. Ft. an pt. BLACKBURN M.G.C. at D. Sqdn Major H.P. Rayland rejoins from leave.	WWS
	17/3/18		Routine.	WWS

Army Form C. 2118

WAR DIARY
or
INTELLIGENCE SUMMARY.
(*Erase heading not required.*)

Instructions regarding War Diaries and Intelligence Summaries are contained in F. S. Regs., Part II. and the Staff Manual respectively. Title pages will be prepared in manuscript.

Place	Date	Hour	Summary of Events and Information	Remarks and references to Appendices
	18/3/18		Routine	W.J.
	19/3/18		Routine.	W.J.
	20/3/18		Routine	W.J.
	21/3/18	10 PM 10·45 PM	Last train load of 4th and 5th Cavalry Division (Indian Personnel) left SALEUX station. 4th Cav. Div. ceases to exist as such. 20 lorries detailed very urgently to report to Cavalry Corps at once. D.D.S.T. 5th Army rang up to say that the Column had been placed at his disposal and that all available lorries were required at once to meet certain units owing to tactical situation. 78 lorries turned out by 12·30. (38 for 5th M.R.U. & G "Tyre" Press from HAM - EPPEVILLE road to ROYE)(15 for 3rd Army Troops M.T. Coy MANICOURT)(28 for "F" "Tyre" Press from PERONNE - FLAMICOURT to Sugar Factory at LA FLAQUE.)	W.J.

WAR DIARY
or
INTELLIGENCE SUMMARY.

Army Form C. 2118

Place	Date	Hour	Summary of Events and Information	Remarks and references to Appendices
	22/3/18		Received orders about 6 P.M. from D.D.S.T. 2nd. 5th Army to evacuate SALEUX at once and move to NEUVILLE (CORBIE). SALEUX vacated by 8.30 P.M.	WJJ
	23/3/18	2.20 A.M.	Received 5th Army detail for 30 lorries to proceed at once to MARCELCAVE. Lt. J.E. Andrew returned with his Conv. of 20 lorries from temporary duty with 1st Cav. Div. M.T. Coy. Orders received at 1.15 P.M. from D.D.S.T. 5th Army to recall all lorries out on details, to CORBIE. Lt. Andrew and 20 lorries sent out at 9 P.M. to park on CORBIE - GRAY road at 10.P.M. for duty under 5th Army.	WJJ
	24/3/18		No details in morning. Capt H. Wickham sent with 25 lorries on duty & subsequent orders received for him to command "Q" Convoy. Capt Sealy sent off with 25 lorries to temporarily command "D" Convoy.	WJJ DDST 1089 d 24.3.18.
	25/3/18		Capt Sealy returned about 5 A.M. having handed over div. "D" convoy to Capt McNab, 5th Cav. Sup. Col.	WJJ

WAR DIARY
or
INTELLIGENCE SUMMARY.
(Erase heading not required.)

Army Form C. 2118.

Place	Date	Hour	Summary of Events and Information	Remarks and references to Appendices
	26/3/18		Received orders at 10.0 AM 15 move Column from NEUVILLE (GR 15/15) 15 REVELLES (S.W. of AMIENS.) Continued issuing of pamphlets, orders for 5/5 Army Day for movement of troops.	MMB
	27/3/18		Following Secret Documents destroyed by fire on account of their being no longer required:- Code Letters for Ammunition Railhead & Reserves, Supply & 4th B (groups), Code names of units of 4th Cav. Div. G.1/3/13; d/20/5/17; G.1/3/15 d/26/5/17 G.1/3/18 d/20/5/17; & 1/3/24 d/17/3/17; G.107/4 d/13/6/17. Chap showing Corps and Divisional Boundaries, copy No.72, issued to Major H.P.Raymond ASC on 6/6/17. Copy of nineteen contained in 4th Cav. Div. G/107/33 d/17-9-17, together with Cavalry Corps Station Code Calls, 4th Cav. Div. G/107/36, copies No.299, and 4th Cav. Div. G/107/35 Cavalry Corps Code Names copy No. 149, & G/107/37. Organization Tables for 4th Cav. Div. (Q. 4.5.8.) d/18/11/17. The ADS 426 (Registered Letters) for the following Divisions were destroyed, the necessary eight months having elapsed, 11-12-6 to 15-2-17, 15-2-17 to 18-4-17, 18-4-17 to 14-7-17. all available lorries employed on 5th Army Convoys.	MMB

WAR DIARY
or
INTELLIGENCE SUMMARY.
(Erase heading not required.)

Army Form C. 2118

Place	Date	Hour	Summary of Events and Information	Remarks and references to Appendices
	28+29/3/18		All available Lorries (Nos 7) employed on 5th Army Convoys.	WW.
	30/3/18		3 Postal Lorries returned to duty from 4th & 5th Cav. Div. Post office as no longer required. All available Lorries (Nos 6) still away on 5th Army Convoys. The following officers still away on Lorrey duties for 5th Army :— Capt N. Wickham, Lt R.O.D. Clatterton, Lieut E.L. Ogilthorpe, & Lieut J.C. Andrew, "21" H.W. Franck. Lieut J.F.B. Ashton still our detachment at MARSEILLES north 30 Lorries.	WW.
		8.30 P.M.	Driver and mate of L.G.O.C lorry W.D.No. 6259. (Col. No. 143) reported back in port. This lorry having broken down on 27th whilst on duty with 5th Army Convoys. (A.M. "A") Lorry kept by them at MORISEL on 29th. Wide report attached. Also handed in a note to the effect that lorry 3519 L.G.O. had been rejoined by 50th Division for signal work.	
	31/3/18		duty. The position as regards Lorries at 6 P.M. as far as known was as follows :— Available 11. Under Repair 4. Awaiting satisfying 1. With DADSS	

Army Form C. 2118

WAR DIARY
or
INTELLIGENCE SUMMARY
(Erase heading not required.)

Place	Date	Hour	Summary of Events and Information	Remarks and references to Appendices
			4th & 5th Cav. Divs. 10. Direction of Agriculture 5th Army 1. Abandoned on 29th. 1. At MARSEILLES 30. 50th Division Signals 1. 5th Army TRPS M.T. Coy 13. 5th Army Convoys 66. Lieut. Wratlin 13. Wanting to complete 1. Stee out on Company duty 3. Wireless 4, Stores 4 = total 160. Instructions received from DDST Fifth Army not to attempt to collect lorry 6259 from MORISEL for the present, matter to be put forward again in a week's time.	

H.P. Raymond
MAJOR.
O.C. 4th CAVALRY SUP. COL.

4TH CAVALRY SUPPLY COLUMN.
No.

APPENDIX

Statement regarding the loss of Lorry W.D. No. 6239 (L.G.
on 29-3-18.

M1/6657 Pte. West G.A. states :-
On the night of March 27th my lorry (L.G.O.C. 6259)
one of a convoy of 20 lorries moving Canadian troops from the direction
of BRETEUIL up to VILLERS BRETONNEUX.

On passing through FOUNCON my lorry broke down with
differential trouble, and was taken in tow by another lorry as far as
the fork roads S.W. of MORISEL. Here the troops in my lorry were off-
loaded and put into another lorry by Capt. Wickham who said he would
send a lorry back to me later on to tow me back to the lines.

My mate and I remained there with the lorry until about
9 p.m. 29th. Whilst waiting we asked nearly every lorry that passed and
several transport officers, to tow us back but they all refused owing
to their being already overloaded.

On the night of the 28th I asked a staff officer who was
looking after some transport, if he could get a lorry to tow me away.
He said it was impossible and that we should stop there as long as we
could and then set fire to the lorry before leaving it.

About midday 29th the Germans started shelling very
heavily all round us and when it was getting dusk a French Officer
told me that the troops we could see coming out of the wood on the
ridge in front were Germans. When it began to get dusk I asked a
British Infantry Officer what I ought to do, and he told me to set
fire to the lorry and get away. I asked him if he would give me an
order in writing to do this but he said that there was no need for it
in times like these. About half an hour later I asked an officer, who
was in charge of some Machine Guns which had taken up a position near
the lorry, what I ought to do, and he said that we were on no account
to set fire to the lorry as it would give his position away. He said
we should break the lorry up as much as possible and get away.

We then destroyed the plugs, water pipes, and radiator,
and took the magneto away with us. We tried to break up the cylinders
but could not as they broke the hammer we were using.

Later on we passed a lorry belonging to the 7th D.W.C.
Reserve M.T. Coy. on the road to AILLY sur NOYE, broken down with
magneto trouble. I handed over my magneto to them and obtained a
receipt for it.

We reported back to the Column at about 8 p.m. 30th.

(M1/6657 Pte. West G.A.)   West G.A.
                                                          31-3-18.
I corroborate the above statement.

(M2/077195 Pte. Ramsden J.L.)   Ramsden J.L.
                                                          31-3-18.

At daybreak on 31-3-18, I sent a motor cyclist (M2/018512 Pte.
Newman F.J.) to see if it would be possible to get a lorry up to MORISEL
to tow 6259 away. He reported back at 10.30 a.m. to say that the Germans
were just the other side of MORISEL and that nothing was allowed to go
(except on foot) beyond AILLY sur NOYE, except Ambulances which were
allowed as far as the turning up to MORISEL.

D.D.S.T. 5th Army was asked for authority to send up a lorry to
MORISEL to attempt a rescue. (Copy of letter attached).

                                                          Major.
                                        O.C. 4th Cav. Sup. Col.
12 noon.
31-3-18.

(Copy).

D.D.S.T. Fifth Army.
───────────

It was reported to me last night that one of my lorries (L.G.O. 6259.) having broken down at MORISEL on the night of the 27th, had to be abandoned by its driver on the night of the 29th owing to the close proximity of the Germans.

The driver broke up or removed the most vital parts in order to render the lorry useless before coming away.

I am of opinion that this lorry might even now be got away by towing it, under cover of darkness.

The chief difficulty is, however, that nothing is allowed to go beyond AILLY SUR NOYE.

Can the necessary authority be granted please to run a lorry up at night to MORISEL to attempt a rescue of the abandoned lorry, which is approximately one mile behind the line as it was this morning early.

(Signed) H.P. Raymond, Major.
O.C. 4th Cav.Sup.Col.
───────────

12 noon.
31-3-18.
───────────

(Copy)

O. 4th Cav.Sup.Col.
―――――――――

At the present moment, it being of primary importance to keep forward roads clear, no efforts should be made to salve the lorry. Bring this matter up in a week's time please.

(Signed) M.Shaw Page, Major.
for D.D.S.T. Fifth Army.
―――――――――

31-3-18.
―――――

www.ingramcontent.com/pod-product-compliance
Lightning Source LLC
Chambersburg PA
CBHW081556160426
43191CB00011B/1947